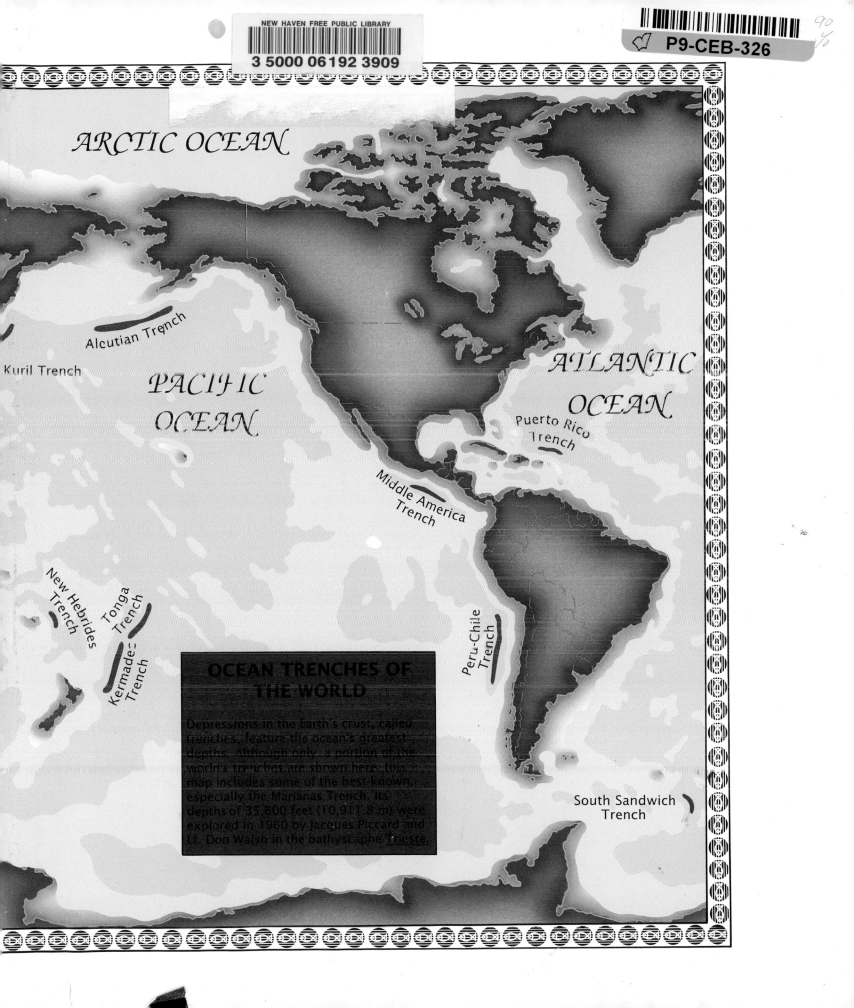

ARCTIC OCEAN

Aleutian Trench

Kuril Trench

PACIFIC OCEAN

ATLANTIC OCEAN

Puerto Rico Trench

Middle America Trench

New Hebrides Trench

Tonga Trench

Kermadec Trench

Peru-Chile Trench

OCEAN TRENCHES OF THE WORLD

Depressions in the Earth's crust, called trenches, feature the ocean's greatest depths. Although only a portion of the world's trenches are shown here, this map includes some of the best-known, especially the Marianas Trench. Its depths of 35,800 feet (10,911.8 m) were explored in 1960 by Jacques Piccard and Lt. Don Walsh in the bathyscaphe *Trieste*.

South Sandwich Trench

WINDOW
ON THE
DEEP

The Adventures of

UNDERWATER EXPLORER

Sylvia Earle

BY ANDREA CONLEY

A New England Aquarium Book

FRANKLIN WATTS
New York • London • Toronto • Sydney
1991

This book is dedicated to the marine biologists of the world—for their concern for and care of our oceans and the creatures that live there. Those scientists who have been personally and professionally inspiring know who they are.

Acknowledgments

This book would not have been possible without the wonderful support and guidance of Dr. Sylvia Earle, who has been a great inspiration. Thanks also to Ken Mallory, Margaret Thompson, Dan Guidera, and Chris Conley for their encouragement, support, and editorial direction. As always, the staff of the New England Aquarium has offered endless advice and information. Specifically, the author extends warm gratitude to Sandra Goldfarb, Vikki Corliss, Greg Early, Dan Laughlin, Sue Knapp, Holly Martel, John Dayton, Dr. Bill Robinson, Steve Spina, and Manisha Gambhir.

World map endsheets by Joe Le Monnier / Diagrams by Lloyd Paul Birmingham

Front cover: Sylvia Earle swims with a spotted dolphin named Sandy. (Inset: a jellyfish). *Back cover:* Sylvia gets acquainted with a moray eel. *Frontispiece:* Sylvia maneuvers the submersible *Deep Rover* on a test dive 50 feet (15.2 m) down in the waters of the Bahamas.

Photographs copyright © : David Doubilet: pp.1, 19 top left, 19 bottom right, 20 bottom left, 30, 35; Ocean Images: pp. 4, 7, 9 (all Charles Nicklin), 5, 6, 11 bottom, 13, 14, 16, 17, 19 top right, 19 bottom left, 20 top, 20 bottom right, 28 top right, 29 bottom left, 33 (all Al Giddings), 8 (Walt Clayton), 10 (Pete Romano), 11 top (Daniel Nord); Deep Ocean Engineering: pp. 22, 25 left, 27; Jeff Mangiat: p. 32; NASA: p. 34; all other photographs copyright © Sea Studios, Inc.

The quotes attributed to Sylvia Earle on pages 7 and 12, and most of the information in the "Appendix: Highlights of Diving History" were taken from *Exploring the Deep Frontier, The Adventure of Man in the Sea.* Copyright © 1980 by Sylvia A. Earle and Al Giddings. Reprinted by permission of the publisher, National Geographic Society.

Library of Congress Cataloging-in-Publication Data

Conley, Andrea,
    Window on the deep: the adventures of underwater explorer Sylvia Earle / by Andrea Conley.
    p. cm.
    "A New England Aquarium book"
    Includes bibliographical references and index.
    Summary: Describes the underwater exploration of Sylvia Earle, the woman who has set many of the current diving records.
    ISBN 0-531-11119-9 (lib. ed.) — ISBN 0-531-15232-4
    1. Underwater exploration. Juvenile literature. 2. Diving, Submarine—Juvenile literature. 3. Earle, Sylvia A. 1935—Juvenile literature. [1. Underwater exploration. 2. Diving, Submarine. 3. Earle, Sylvia A., 1935- .] I. Title. GC65.C65   1991
551.46'0092 dc20
[B]
                    91-17792   CIP AC

Contents

Chapter One
EXPL⭐RING
THE EDGE OF
THE ABYSS

Sylvia Earle hit the rugged, sloping terrain with a thump.

Her journey was over. Here, on the floor of the Pacific Ocean, she was standing where no human had ever stood before. Dressed in a large white armor suit, her human presence seemed out of place in an indigo world full of strange aquatic life forms.

On September 19, 1979, Sylvia stood 1,250 feet (381 m) below the sparkling surface of the Hawaiian waters 6 miles (9.7 km) off the island of Oahu, the first person to walk so deeply underwater unconnected to surface support. Considering the remoteness of the place and the difficulties it presented to human explorers, Sylvia could well have been on the moon.

Getting to the deep ocean was no easy task. Sylvia had descended nearly as deeply as the Empire State Building is high, in a feat that would earn her the nickname "Her Royal Deepness." She began the voyage strapped to a platform on the front of a small submarine named *Star II*. Only upon alighting on the ocean floor did she free herself from the submarine's platform to have a look around.

Facing page: Sylvia, protected by the pressure-resistant Jim suit,
hangs from a cable tethered to submarine Star II,
which is floating near the surface. Another diver monitors the process.

*Sylvia Earle stands in front of the submersible Star II which
will take her on a record dive 1,250 feet (381 m) deep
in waters off the island of Oahu, Hawaii.*

A garland of flowers decorates the helmet of the Jim suit that will take Sylvia to record depths. Sylvia's only connection to a life-support safety vehicle will be to Star II, the yellow submarine in the background.

Sylvia explored while *Star II* followed close behind. For safety reasons, she remained tethered to the submarine by a black communications cable for the entire dive. Together they resembled an alien with its mechanical dog on a leash, a twosome out for a nighttime stroll.

Sylvia maneuvered the stiff shell of her diving suit. It was called a Jim suit after its first user, a diver named Jim Jarratt. Sylvia took small steps along the ocean floor. Moving had been awkward at first, but after a week's training she could walk, turn, lie down, get up, and even, she had recalled, "manage a slow-motion cha cha." The oil-filled joints of the suit enabled its occupant to move in spite of the deep-ocean pressure.

Sylvia Earle smiles for the camera before her Jim suit helmet is sealed.

Although she was accustomed to her cumbersome gear, Sylvia didn't like the way it restricted her. She was used to the dolphin-like freedom of diving with a Self-Contained Underwater Breathing Apparatus, better known as SCUBA. With SCUBA, she was weightless and agile and breathed air through a mouthpiece connected to a small tank on her back. But the deep ocean presents special problems to divers. SCUBA is not an option there.

Like the moon, the deep ocean is inhospitable to humans. We cannot remain underwater without taking air with us. The water is painfully cold and dark without the sun's warmth, and water pressure at great depths would be fatal without proper protection. Crushing water pressure would cause the air spaces to burst in the lungs, ears, and sinuses. The only way to venture into the remote habitat of the deep ocean is to literally seal ourselves into a capsule containing our own environment.

Like the suits worn by astronauts, the Jim protects its wearer from outside conditions while supplying normal air to breathe and maintaining comfortable temperatures. The suit's thick walls provide heavy-duty protection in the shape of a human body. The suit's magnesium alloy construction shields its wearer from the heavy water pressure in the deep ocean.

Perched on the deck of a catamaran (not visible here), Sylvia begins her record-breaking descent in the Jim suit attached to the submarine Star II. Scuba divers make certain that the beginning of the dive takes place without any problems and that none of their equipment gets tangled.

Below: *Sylvia's descent continues as they go deeper in their quest for a record depth dive in 1979.*
Facing page (top): *Divers release the Jim suit and Star II from the deck of the catamaran so they can continue the descent without it.* Facing page (bottom): *A practice run in shallow water shows how Sylvia will set out on her own during her record-setting dive.*

The Jim suit's ability to resist water pressure gave Sylvia a lot to be thankful for. Where she now stood she was protected from about 600 pounds (272.2 kg) of water pressure on each and every inch of the Jim suit. On land, we experience about 14.7 pounds (6.7 kg) of constant, or "atmospheric," pressure all over our bodies. That amount increases another 14.7 pounds (6.7 kg) for each 33 feet (10.1 m) that a diver descends underwater. The Jim suit's sturdy construction bore the pressure at 1,250 feet (381 m) with no signs of stress.

Sylvia felt a warm glow of excitement as she concentrated on her surroundings. Although the ocean floor was as strange and remote as the moon, there was one big difference. The moon is a lonely place completely devoid of life. But here there was life at every turn. The deep ocean teems with a wonderful array of odd and colorful creatures, many of which are more bizarre than anything depicted in space-alien movies.

Sylvia peered from one of the Jim's heavy plastic portholes to see a field of tiny tentacled animals called bamboo coral. When she touched one of these corals with Jim's steel "hand," pulses of blue light beamed up from the coral's base on the sea floor.

Intrigued by the light show, Sylvia pulled her arms out of the large arms of her suit as if she had been pulling them from the sleeves of an overcoat. With her arms free to move within the walls of the Jim, she jotted a description in her notebook: "I am in the middle of some strange looking spirals of bamboo coral," she wrote, "and near a broad, pale frond of soft coral so crowded with white polyps that it resembles a pear tree in full flower." These descriptions came easily to Sylvia. She had made a habit of recording her adventures on paper ever since she'd first observed wildlife in the pond behind her childhood home in New Jersey.

Here in her deep-sea garden Sylvia marveled at all the different critters she saw. Sylvia often uses the word "critters" to describe the plants and animals she encounters on her adventures. Her list for the Jim dive included:

• "an eighteen-inch [45.7 cm]-long shark, dark above, pale below with luminous green eyes . . .
• "a dozen or so long-legged bright red galathied crabs swaying on the branches of a pink sea fan;
• "a small, sleek, dark brown lantern fish darting by with lights glistening along its sides;

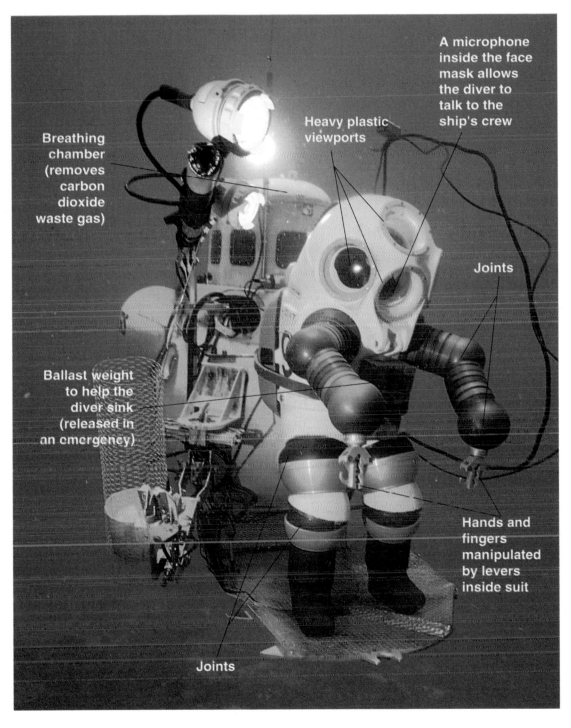

Breathing chamber (removes carbon dioxide waste gas)

A microphone inside the face mask allows the diver to talk to the ship's crew

Heavy plastic viewports

Joints

Ballast weight to help the diver sink (released in an emergency)

Hands and fingers manipulated by levers inside suit

Joints

THE JIM SUIT

Sylvia prepares to step off a small platform at the front of the submersible Star II so she is free to explore the ocean floor.

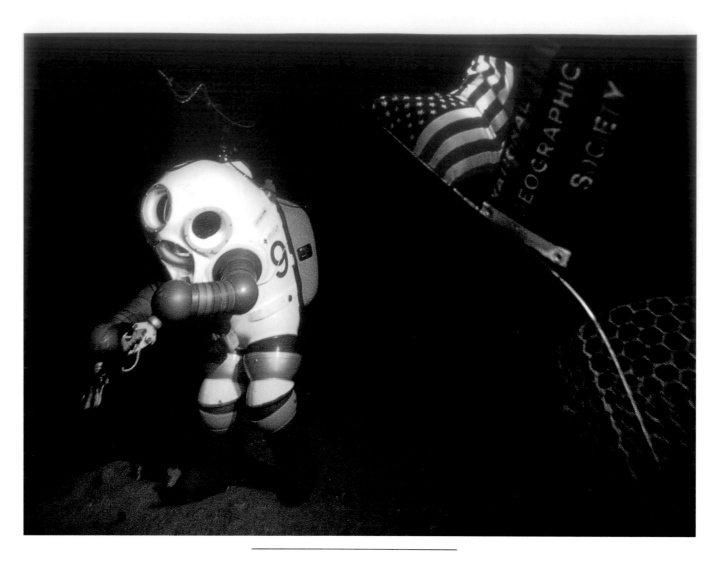

Sylvia unfurls the American flag during her record-setting dive.

- "an orange fish and several plumelike sea pens clinging to the rocky bottom near the edge of visibility . . . and
- "sparks of living light, blue green flashes of small transparent creatures brushing against my faceplate."

Sylvia knew from experience that the deep sea is not as dark as people think. The light there comes not from the sun but from some of the animals that live there. Many of them glow and flash, illuminating their way through the water with natural lights like underwater fireflies. This natural light is called bioluminescence.

Caught up in her fascination with everything around her, Sylvia often lost track of time when exploring a new place. Only the crackle of a voice over the radio broke her concentration. "Sylvia, it's time to go up," said Al Giddings, who was keeping his eye on her from the window of *Star II.* Al and Sylvia had planned the Jim dive together and were in constant radio contact during the dive to ensure Sylvia's safety. "You've been out there two and a half hours," Al reminded her. Reluctantly, Sylvia prepared for her ascent.

Star II powered its engines and began to rise slowly. Sylvia waited for it to pull her from above, the vertical likeness of a water skier waiting for a tow behind a boat. Gently the submarine hovered overhead and lifted her from the ocean floor. Sylvia dangled under the black communications cable like a puppet on a string. She watched the pale, craggy seascape she had just explored disappear into the deep ocean's navy ink. Gradually she and *Star II* approached the water's surface.

Sylvia looked through her faceplate and watched the dark water fade to the familiar aquamarine of shallower tropical waters. Looking into the crystal water reminded Sylvia of the swimming pool where she got her first clear look underwater. She remembered the precious gift of a pair of goggles she was given for her twelfth birthday. Sylvia had first tried them on in her backyard swimming pool in New Jersey. Like the Jim's faceplate, the goggles were Sylvia's window into the world of water.

A cloud of foamy bubbles made by the submarine's thrusters dispersed as Sylvia and *Star II* finally broke the water's surface. Sylvia's first sight was the research ship named *Aloha,* a Hawaiian word meaning hello. Sylvia squinted into the sun. She'd grown accustomed to its absence in the dark world below. She bobbed in the water surrounded by the lush Hawaiian mountains. Sylvia waited to be hoisted by a strong crane onto the research ship's deck. Although the air in the Jim made her float, she and the suit would weigh a hefty ½ ton (453.6 kg) outside the water.

While she waited, Sylvia considered what she and her colleagues had just accomplished. She was certain the dive marked a new period of oceanic exploration. They had proven that the Jim suit, which had been used primarily for work on oil rigs, could also be used for scientific exploration. The group's accomplishment inspired Sylvia. When she finally landed on the ship's deck, Al Giddings unsealed the Jim helmet. As Sylvia climbed out of her suit she asked, "So when do I get to go deeper?"

Chapter Two
THE UNDERWATER
HOTEL

Sylvia's question came as no surprise to Al. He often teased that Sylvia was more comfortable underwater than she was on land. As one of Sylvia's regular diving companions, Al knew that Sylvia had spent nearly 6,000 hours—nearly one year of her life—underwater. During the time he'd known her, Sylvia had been on hundreds of aquatic adventures. She had lived in underwater habitats, each a kind of underwater hotel with its own supply of air, where divers can enter and leave as they wish. In one adventure, Sylvia had led the first all-women's team of aquanauts. For nearly two weeks the group, using SCUBA, had lived underwater and conducted scientific studies from a base at a specially equipped underwater hotel.

But to Sylvia these adventures were mainly a means to an end. As a scientist, diving enabled her to study the creatures of the sea in their own realm, to use the ocean as a laboratory. She had been diving since 1953, just ten years after SCUBA was first invented by the industrial engineer Emile Gagnan and the undersea explorer Jacques-Yves Cousteau. She first used the system, known then as the Aqua-Lung, when she

---

Facing page: *Some of Sylvia's fondest memories of ocean diving are from encounters with dolphins and other whales. The Atlantic spotted dolphin shown here in the Bahamas is named Sandy. To Sylvia, one of the most important ways to understand animals is to get to know them on their own terms—underwater.*

was studying to be a marine biologist at Florida State University. It was after her first dive using SCUBA that Sylvia realized how important it would be to her work.

Diving enabled Sylvia to study and explore underwater plants and animals right where they lived—and she came to know a lot of them. Al often referred to her as the underwater equivalent of Dr. Doolittle, the storybook veterinarian who could communicate with animals. During their dives together Al had seen Sylvia swim with whales and dolphins, befriend tiny crabs, and scratch the bellies of huge sharks.

Al had often observed the infectious power of Sylvia's interest in marine life. He'd watched her convert many a landlubber into a marine enthusiast. She'd work her magic on them. "Anyone can get acquainted with the plants and animals in the ocean, or in rivers, or in lakes," she'd say. "You don't have to go into the deep ocean to do it. It's simple. Just get a face mask, put it on, and look into the water. We have the joy of getting to know the planet Earth from the inside out."

The critters Sylvia had met underwater had made her increasingly aware of the uniqueness of the planet Earth and its declining condition. Besides Dr. Doolittle, Sylvia had also been likened to Dr. Seuss's fictional character the Lorax, who spoke out against the destruction of forests. Sylvia's concern for the ocean's plants and animals was as strong as the Lorax's concern for trees. She often warned of man's harm to the oceans—pollution, overfishing, overbuilding in coastal areas—reminding people of the need to take care of the planet. "Each plant and animal, no matter how small, is somehow important to the Earth's whole system," she would say.

Sylvia and Al had had long conversations about the oceans. Sylvia convinced Al that the oceans and their inhabitants were what made Earth special. Both were painfully aware that scientists still knew little about the ocean. They agreed that studying the ocean was essential to understanding the workings of the planet as a healthy system. "Like doctors who must first study normal human anatomy, we need to know

Sylvia believes underwater divers can make good ambassadors for the ocean and the creatures that live there. By sharing their experiences, divers can teach all of us to care for sea life. Counterclockwise from top right: Sylvia Earle becomes acquainted with jellyfish from Micronesia's Truk Lagoon, a moray eel, a sea snake in the Coral Sea, and a school of small mouth grunts.

how the Earth and its oceans work when they're healthy so we can fix them when they're not," Sylvia would say.

Al remembered how Sylvia's persuasive talents had helped raise money for the Jim dive. Now, as he watched Sylvia climb out from Jim's large, white shell, Al was sure that Sylvia Earle would find a way to probe the ocean depths even deeper.

Counterclockwise, from top right: *Sylvia is pictured here swimming with a spotted dolphin; one of Sylvia's lifelong loves in the ocean is the scientific study of marine plants like the mass of algae she is collecting here in Truk Lagoon, Micronesia. Sylvia even has a plant named after her called* Plinia earlii; *Sylvia's curiosity takes her into a giant basket sponge to explore what she can find inside; Sylvia returns to the beach after a dive during which she collected specimens of plants and animals. She will later study these in the laboratory.*

Chapter Three

A SUBMERSIBLE NAMED

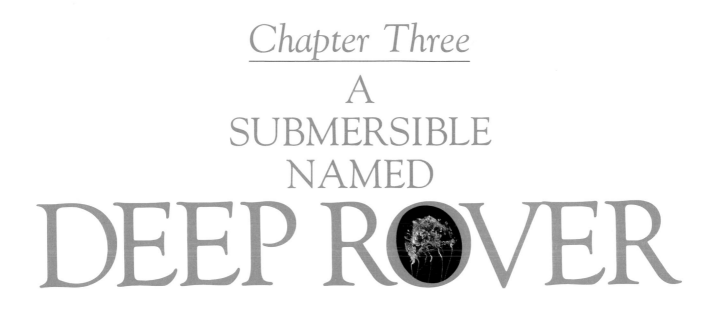

DEEP ROVER

Although Sylvia had set a new record for deep-ocean exploration by taking the Jim suit to its limit, it was only a small step in a long journey. A two-and-one-half-hour dive at 1,250 feet (381 m) in a vast and little-explored ocean was like "shining a small flashlight into a large dark forest," Sylvia once said. But, since few tools existed to take her to the depths she dreamed about, Sylvia took matters into her own hands. She called someone she knew could help.

During the Jim dive, Sylvia had met a British technical wizard named Graham Hawkes. He was the engineer who helped design the suit, tailoring its functions to Sylvia's needs as a scientist. Her instincts told her that if anyone could design a submersible to go deeper, it was Hawkes.

Sylvia and Graham made a great team. As a scientist looking for ways to work in the sea, Sylvia presented a man who loved to unravel engineering puzzles with a long list of problems to solve. Together they set out to create a submersible unlike all others. Most submersibles

---

Facing page: *Surrounded by the submersible* Deep Rover's *acrylic plastic sphere 5 inches (12.7 cm) thick, Sylvia has an almost unlimited view of the deep-sea creatures around her. In* Rover, *she descended 3,000 feet (914.4 m) to break her own solo diving record at the time.*

were too expensive to use regularly for scientific research. They were heavy and required a large mother ship with an equally large staff to transport them to the exploration site, then move them in and out of the water. There were other technical problems. Most submersibles had small portholes, making it difficult to observe animal life. None were very well equipped for specimen collecting, and all required long hours of training to learn to operate.

The new submersible would be lightweight, battery-operated, and simple and inexpensive to use. Instead of small portholes typical of most submersibles, the vehicle itself would be a transparent sphere and thus provide excellent all-around views of sea life. It would have easy-to-operate manipulator arms and a suction device, or "slurp gun," for examining and collecting aquatic plants and animals.

Nearly five years had passed since Sylvia's historic Jim dive. Now, 60 miles (96.6 km) off the coast of San Diego, California, Sylvia climbed into a vehicle resembling a space-age car without wheels. Among its main features were a 5-inch (12.7-cm)-thick acrylic plastic sphere to enclose and protect its operator. It also had two long, black arms; the left one contained a large suction cup for collecting specimens, and the right one contained steel grabbers for examining animals underwater. The arms could be manipulated using switches on the submersible's control panel.

It was clear from the spherical shape of the submersible that Graham had not forgotten Sylvia's first priority. Tests had shown that spheres withstand the water pressure of the deep ocean better than any other shape. The vehicle, christened *Deep Rover,* could take Sylvia to 3,000 feet (914.4 m)—more than twice the depth she'd been to with the Jim suit. Like the Jim, *Deep Rover*'s atmospheric system would provide a steady supply of air for Sylvia, its lone occupant, to breathe. The submersible would also insulate her from the near freezing waters of the deep sea. Sylvia liked to say that *Deep Rover* was really just a large diving suit with many of the conveniences of a house.

It was sunset when a large crane on the deck of the vessel *Egabrag III* lifted Sylvia and *Deep Rover* over the ship's edge. *Egabrag III* was a 140-foot (42.7-m) research ship named after an old Navy garbage barge. Egabrag is "garbage" spelled backwards, the ship's captain told Sylvia.

When *Deep Rover* touched down into the water, Sylvia was full of the

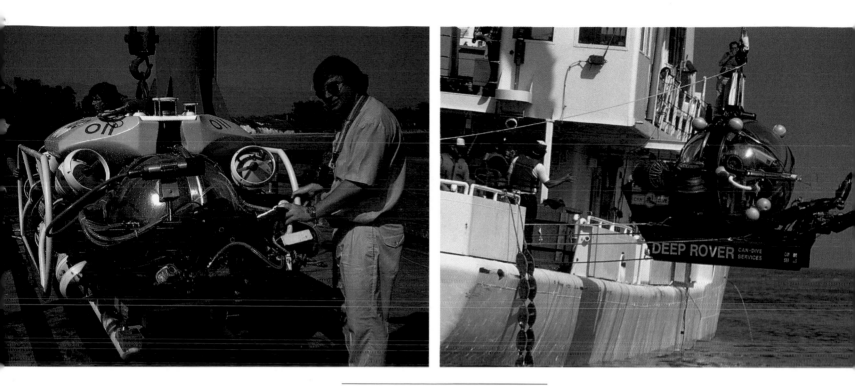

Left: *Engineer and designer Graham Hawkes stands in front of* Deep Rover, *the submersible he designed with Sylvia Earle and members of Deep Ocean Engineering.*
Right: Deep Rover *is launched for a record dive by a whip's winch, which places it gently into the water. While other submersibles have tiny portholes from which to observe life in the depths,* Deep Rover *has a clear all-round view.*

same anticipation she always felt at the start of a new adventure. Then she powered the submersible's thrusters and dropped slowly into the sea like a sinking ship.

Down Sylvia went. It would take about an hour to reach 3,000 feet (914.4 m). She reported her progress to the topside crew by radio. About thirty minutes into the dive she announced, "I am at 1,343 feet [409.3 m]; the ocean bottom here slopes gently downward." Then a bit later, "I've reached 2,000 feet [609.6 m] . . . Two small sharks just darted by . . . Here comes the 2,700 mark [823 m]. . . ."

When Sylvia reached 3,000 feet (914.4 m), she broke her own record for deep solo diving. The record, however, was not on her mind. She was too busy radioing a narrative of her sightings to the team at the surface. "I see a beautiful red octopus, a lantern fish, and a see-through octopus with long tentacles." When Sylvia turned off *Deep Rover*'s lights, her eyes beheld the deep-sea fireworks she found so interesting. Jelly

animals illuminated themselves to parade their various shapes. Fish glowed with light. The show went on and on.

Sylvia basked in the pleasure of having such wonderful critters greet her. She was always impressed by the individuality of the animals she encountered. She took a moment to recall one of her favorites, a small crab she had seen on one of her earlier dives. She had described it for Graham as part of a discussion that resulted in *Deep Rover*. "It was carrying a tiny bouquet of coral in its hind legs, who knows why. If I hadn't been in that animal's own home, I would never have known that it does such a thing," she said.

From her current position at 3,000 feet (914.4 m), Sylvia turned her attention to the geography of the place. The abyss below her seemed unfathomable. The deepest part of the ocean still lay almost 6½ miles (10.5 km) below. Sylvia thought of all the mountains and trenches below, waiting to be explored. Challenged by the thought, she vowed to revisit this amazing world by finding a way to reach the very bottom of the ocean.

The diagram on the facing page represents life-forms that can be found in the Pacific Ocean. The animals are not drawn to scale because of the great range of sizes. Characteristic depths are indicated in the right margin of the drawing.

Sylvia's quest for the ocean's depths is inspired by her curiosity to learn more about wildlife, like the crab shown here carrying what looks like an underwater bouquet.

Creatures of the Deep

Deepwater animals brought back by submersibles and other collecting devices reflect the vast diversity of underwater life. (a) This flatfish began life with one eye on each side of its body. It has now changed into an animal with both eyes on one side in preparation for its life lying at the bottom of the ocean. (b) In the early stages of its life, a Pacific lamprey eel looks very little like the way it will appear as an adult. Such animals drift in ocean currents as they feed and grow. (c) The eel pout is a bottom-dwelling fish. Brought up from the depths of the ocean, it instinctively curls its body in response to the bright light. (d) The gulper eel is well-adapted to life in the deep sea, often living in bitter cold depths of 9,000 feet (2,743.2 m) or more. Sometimes called "all-mouths," gulper eels try to seize whatever comes along as food. (e) Such deep-sea worms are an important food source for other animals of the deep. Feathery appendages may help it wriggle through the water. (f) The deep-sea anglerfish waves a glowing lure in front of its mouth to entice potential food closer for a better look. In the deep ocean, as many as 90 percent of the creatures sparkle, flash, or glow. (g) Pictured here is a vivid red deepwater shrimp. These shrimp often glow and move up and down a thousand feet or more in the water each day. (h) The box medusa or sea wasp is nearly transparent, and its tentacles contain powerful stinging cells to stun or kill its prey. (i) The discovery of microscopic plankton reinforces Sylvia's observation that "there is life in every teaspoon of water." (j) This species of jellyfish from the Pacific and Indian Oceans is relatively rare and seldom seen. Its body, which moves by slow contractions, can reach a width of nearly ¾ inch (18 mm).

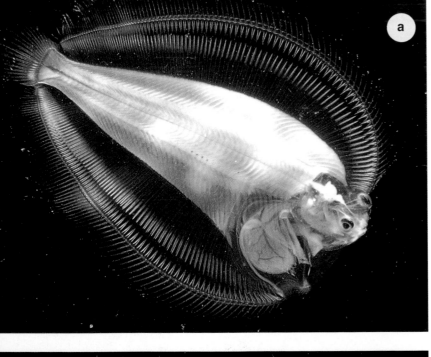

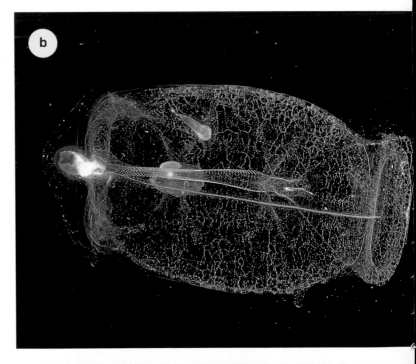

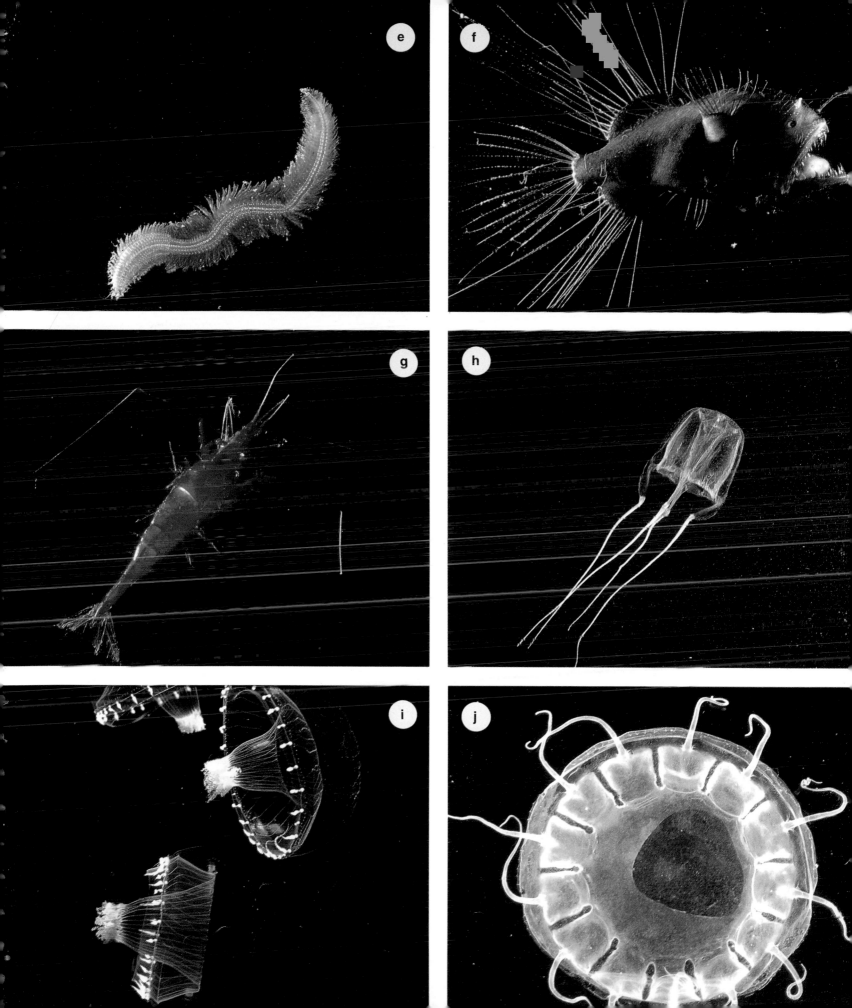

Chapter Four

ONWARD
AND
DOWNWARD

A staff of nine works diligently in a hangar-shaped building in San Leandro, California. They hover over a long fiberglass capsule with wings. Graham Hawkes directs the group in the creation of one of two new submersibles named *Deep Flight I* and *Deep Flight II*. The submersibles are another step toward Sylvia's goal to explore the deepest part of the ocean.

The building that houses the submersibles is occupied by Deep Ocean Engineering, a company Sylvia and Graham founded to develop new tools for oceanic work and exploration. A glimpse around the place reveals the company's latest endeavors. A small underwater robot called *Phantom* floats in a test pool. It is called an ROV, short for "remotely operated vehicle," like the one used to explore the wreck of the ill-fated luxury liner the *Titanic*. *Deep Flight*'s parts clutter the floor while the work is in progress. A large conference room reveals drawings and plans for a number of exciting projects.

Deep Flight I and *II*, which are both underwater gliders, are nearly complete. The conference room plans reveal they will go faster and deeper than *Deep Rover*. They offer Sylvia new opportunities to com-

---

Facing page: *Sylvia gets acquainted with a moray eel. "Once you've looked a fish in the eye, you realize 'that fish is looking at me.' Who's being inspected, who's the watcher, and who's the watchee?"*

mune with aquatic animals. Each *Deep Flight* is capable of doing 12 knots, or 13.8 miles (22.2 km) per hour, a brisk pace for a submarine. At this speed, the speed of the fastest whale, Sylvia can frolic among schools of whales, tuna, and squid. *Deep Flight* will enable scientists to learn a great deal about the lives of these elusive animals. When she and Graham test the submersibles together off Monterey, California, they will be 1,000 feet (304.8 m) closer to the deep ocean floor.

In Sylvia's mind, the submersibles will serve another function. *Deep Flight I* and *II* will test principles developed for her favorite project of all: *Ocean Everest.* Graham is designing a submersible that will reach the

---

Facing page: Sylvia swims among a school of jellyfish in Micronesia's Truk Lagoon. "We must realize we are giants where many small creatures live. It is our responsibility to take care of them."

Below: With Deep Flight, *Deep Ocean Engineering is building the world's first underwater aircraft. Packed with technology, the new submersible is expected to blaze the trail for the next assault on the ocean's greatest depths.*

"We humans have to remember that Earth is special," Sylvia cautions. "It is the only planet in the universe that can sustain human life. We need to take care of the planet and the plant and animal life it supports. We just don't know how our carelessness is affecting the Earth's whole system."

deepest-known part of the Pacific Ocean, the Marianas Trench off Guam, which cuts 35,800 feet (10.9 km) into the planet's very core. The trench is 7,000 feet (2.13 km) deeper than Mt. Everest is high. Getting there will fulfill the promise Sylvia made to herself on her 3,000-foot (0.91-km) *Deep Rover* dive.

With *Ocean Everest,* Sylvia could be the Christopher Columbus of the deep ocean. Most of the ocean has not been visited, especially below 20,000 feet (6.1 km), where there is a vast area of unexplored wilderness larger than the United States. Sylvia has a long list of underwater locations she'd like to reach, ranging from underwater ice formations to deep sea volcanoes.

Sylvia is especially interested in the deep trenches, long narrow depressions in the seafloor. Trenches are formed during collisions between pieces of the Earth's crust when one is pushed beneath the other. The greatest depths in the sea are found in trenches, some reaching depths of more than 6½ miles (10.5 km). Like the highest mountain peaks on land, the world's ocean trenches offer some of the greatest challenges. Getting there might well be the closest thing to reaching the center of the Earth.

What is it like to be in one of these trenches? What animals live there? What new understanding of our planet might be had while exploring a deep trench? How might it help us better comprehend the long-term effects of environmental abuse? What might we learn about the origins of life on Earth? Sylvia hopes she will some day be able to answer some of these questions.

Sylvia sees further oceanic exploration as one way to increase everyone's appreciation for the value of the oceans: for the wealth and diversity of life they house, for the food and oxygen they supply, and for the seabeds that may one day supply us with oil and gas. For these reasons, our very destiny is linked to the good health of the oceans.

And where will Sylvia go if she ever finishes exploring the ocean floor? "To the moon," she laughs. But, she quickly adds, "I would love to go, if only to see what the beautiful blue oceans on our planet look like from afar."

Sylvia Earle, underwater explorer and scientist

Appendix
HIGHLIGHTS OF DIVING HISTORY

Fourth century B.C. Early written record of a device for supplying air to divers: Aristotle describes Greek sponge divers breathing air trapped in kettles lowered into the water.

First century B.C. Diving women of the northwestern Pacific gather food from the seafloor during breathhold descents.

1663 Using a diving bell, salvagers recover cannon from the sunken warship *Vasa,* lying 110 feet (33.4 m) down in Stockholm harbor. **(1)**

1690 In England Edmond Halley designs a diving bell that uses weighted barrels lowered from the surface to renew the air supply. Divers later use it to descend more than 50 feet (15.2 m).

1715 Englishman John Lethbridge develops one of the first armored diving dresses—a wooden cylinder with a glass view port and laced leather sleeves—and uses it 60 feet (18.3 m) below. **(2)**

1776 First attack by a military submarine: David Busnell's *Turtle* tries to sink H.M.S. *Eagle* in New York harbor. **(3)**

1819 Appearance of a practical open-dress diving suit fed with pumped air, in England: The invention is generally credited to Augustus Siebe.

1837 Siebe designs an airtight closed-dress diving suit vented by a valve.

1892 Louis Boutan takes the first underwater still photographs, off France. In 1899 he lowers his camera to 165 feet (50.3 m) for successful remote-control pictures. **(4)**

1915 Depth record for recovery of an entire vessel: Salvagers raise the submarine *F-4* from 306 feet (93.3 m) off Honolulu.

1930 Using a bathysphere (a diving sphere for deep-sea observation) , naturalist Dr. William Beebe and designer Otis Barton dive to 1,428 (435.3 m) off Bermuda.

Divers wearing Neufeldt and Kuhnke suits raise 5 tons of gold bullion from the *Egypt,* sunk in 426 feet (129.5 m) of water off France.

1934 The Beebe-Barton bathysphere reaches 3,028 feet (922.9 m) off Bermuda. **(5)**

1935 Jim Jarratt, wearing the "Iron Man" armored suit, locates the sunken *Lusitania,* 330 feet down off Ireland. Modern Jim suits are named for him.

1939 *Squalus* sinks 243 feet (74.1 m) in waters off Portsmouth, New Hampshire; the thirty-three survivors are brought up in the rescue chamber. The *Squalus* is raised during the next four months, marking the first open-sea use of helium as a diving gas. **(6)**

1943 Frenchmen Jacques-Yves Cousteau and Emile Gagnan perfect the fully automatic compressed-air Aqua-Lung and use it to dive to 210 feet (61 m) in the Mediterranean. **(7)**

1945 Arne Zetterström demonstrates the use of hydrogen on a dive to 525 feet (160 m) in the Baltic Sea.

1954 Frenchmen Georges Houot and Pierre Willm pilot the submersible *F.N.R.S. 3* to 13,287 feet (4 km) off Dakar. **(8)**

1960 In the submersible *Trieste,* Jacques Piccard and Lt. Don Walsh of the U.S. Navy, descend to 35,800 feet (10.9 km) in the Marianas Trench, the deepest known place in the sea. **(9)**

1965 Conshelf Three: Six men live 22 days at 328 feet (100 m) in the Mediterranean.

1967 Edwin Link builds *Deep Diver,* the first submersible with an operational lockout chamber.

1968 Perry Oceanographics designs and builds Hydro-Lab, an underwater habitat, off the coast of Florida. **(12)**

1969 Tektite I, sponsored by the U.S. Navy, the U.S. Department of the Interior, and NASA: Four men live for 60 days in 50 feet (15.2 m) of water off the U.S. Virgin Islands.

Submersible *Ben Franklin* drifts in the Gulf Stream for 1,500 miles (2,414 km), reaching depths of 2,000 feet (609.6 m) on its thirty-day journey. Jacques Piccard heads the expedition.

1977 Deepest working saturation dive: Comex divers go to 1,510 feet (.416 m). They later accomplish a record dive to 1,644 feet (0.5 km). **(14)**

1978 Research ship *Glomar Challenger* drills into seafloor sediment through waters 23,104 feet (7 km) deep.

1979 Sylvia Earle, in a Jim suit, dives to 1,250 feet (381 m) off Oahu, riding the submersible *Star II* to the seafloor. **(15)**

1980 Depth of nuclear submarine: Official figure lists depth at more than 400 feet (121.9 m); others estimate more than 1,500 feet (457.2 m). **(16)**

1983 *Deep Rover* launches historic deepest solo dive to 3,000 feet (915.4 m). **(17)**

1989 The ROV *Jason Jr.* is launched from the Woods Hole deep-sea submersible *Alvin* to make its historic exploration of the shipwrecked *Titanic.* **(18)**

The Japanese submersible *Shinkai-6500* reaches its depth limit of 21,320 feet (6,498 km), becoming the world's deepest diving submarine for its time. **(19)**

(15)

(10)

(13)

(14)

(16)

(17)

(5)

1962 Keller and Peter Small use a diving bell to plunge 1,000 feet (304.8 m) off Santa Catalina Island; they breathe a special mix of gases developed by Keller. **(10)**

French bathyscaph *Archimède* dives to 31,308 feet (9.5 km) in the Kuril Trench off Japan.

Man-in-Sea, headed by Edwin A. Link: during this saturation diving project, Belgian Robert Sténuit descends in a decompression chamber to 200 feet (61 m) off the French Riviera and stays 24 hours.

1963 *Trieste* explores the site of the sunken nuclear-powered submarine *Thresher,* at 8,400 feet (2.0 km).

1965 Sealab II: Twenty-eight men remain for fifteen to thirty days at 205 feet (62.5 m) in California waters. **(11)**

1976 Deepest dive in a Jim suit. Oceaneering International's one-atmosphere system goes to 1,440 feet (438.9 m) off Spain to recover a TV cable. **(13)**

Frenchman Jacques Mayol dives to 328 feet (99.4 m) in a breath-hold dive lasting three minutes 40 seconds.

(18)

(8)

(19)

(9)

Glossary

Aquanauts (A-QUA-nots)—undersea explorers; the underwater counterpart to an astronaut, an explorer in space.

Atmospheric **pressure** (at-mah-SPHERE-ik PRESH-ur)—the pressure of air at sea level, about 14.7 (6.6 kg) pounds to the square inch.

Bioluminescence (by-oh-LOO-muh-NES-ens)—a chemical process in living organisms that produces light.

Catamaran—a boat with two parallel hulls shaped like pontoons, which in the case of the Jim suit's support ship, are flooded to let the boat sink below the surface of the water.

Galathied crab (gall-ah-THAY-id)—a relative of the hermit crab, the squat lobster, and the porcelain crab.

Jim suit—a rigid, pressure-resistant diving suit named after its first user, Jim Jarratt. Its limbs move with ball-and-socket joints, and the diver breathes air or oxygen at normal surface pressure.

Knot—1 nautical mile (6,076.115 feet or 1,852 m) per hour.

Lantern fish—small (a big one is 6 inches [15.3 cm] long) deep ocean fishes with two sets of bioluminescent lights, one on the underside of the body and head, and the other near the tail. The tail lights glow especially brightly.

Polyp (POL-up)—a stage in the lives of jellyfish, sea anemones, and corals consisting of a simple stomach with a mouth surrounded by tentacles.

ROV—(to pronounce, sound each letter separately)—remotely operated vehicle. ROVs are unpiloted submersibles that are attached to a support, or mother, ship by a long cable and maneuvered by remote control.

SCUBA (SKOO-bah)—Self-Contained Underwater Breathing Apparatus. Developed in the 1940s, this apparatus allows divers to breathe compressed air while swimming underwater.

Sea fans—soft corals that form flat, branching structures.

Sea pen—a relative of the sea anemone which lives partially buried in sand or mud and extends a plumelike, feathery feeding apparatus to feed on plankton.

Submarine (SUB-muh-reen)—an underwater vehicle first developed as a war machine which is powered today by diesel-electric motors, driven by rechargeable batteries or by nuclear power.

Submersible (sub-MER-sih-bull)—any underwater craft including submarines and remotely operated vehicles (ROVs).

Thrusters—submersible engines that drive propellers and control movement of the ship; besides the tail thruster there are vertical and side thrusters to move the craft up and down or to spin it around.

Trench—underwater depressions in the ocean floor, caused by movement of the Earth's crust. Besides trenches there are huge underwater mountain ranges and vast plains.

Underwater glider—a submersible which has the shape and appearance of a glider, although in the case of *Deep Flight*, it is self-propelled and not dependent on underwater currents for propulsion.

Underwater habitat—a pressurized underwater chamber which divers can enter and leave at will, and where they can live and breathe air for months at a time.

Bibliography

Arkison, Jim. et al., *The Naui Textbook* (Montclair, Calif.: National Association of Underwater Instructors, 1985). All about SCUBA diving: techniques, safety, equipment, and diving physiology.

Asimov, Isaac. *How Did We Find Out About Life in the Deep Sea?* (New York: Walker, 1982). Information about early deep-sea exploration and the marine life found in the deep ocean.

Brownlee, Shannon. "Explorers of Dark Frontiers," *Discover*, February 1986, vol. 7, no. 2, pp. 61–67. Background on Sylvia's record-breaking dive in *Deep Rover*.

Davies, Eryl. *Ocean Frontiers* (London, England: Marshall Cavendish, 1979; New York: Viking Press, 1980). Useful background on diving technology.

The Diagram Group, *Comparisons* (New York: St. Martin's Press, 1980). Good reference for size, distance, and weight comparisons.

Dive to Midnight Waters, BBC television broadcast, 1986.

Earle, Sylvia. "The Lorax Who Speaks for the Fishes," *Radcliffe Quarterly*, September 1990, pp. 2–5. Sylvia's own account of her underwater adventures, education, and scientific career.

Earle, Sylvia. "Ocean Everest—An Idea Whose Time Has Come," *Marine Technology Society Journal*, June 1990, pp. 9–12. More background on Ocean Everest.

Earle, Sylvia A. and Al Giddings, *Exploring the Deep Frontier—The Adventure of Man in the Sea* (Washington, D.C.: National Geographic Society, 1980). An excellent overview of all aspects of oceanic exploration. Includes a detailed account of Sylvia's record-breaking Jim suit dive.

Haupt, Donna E. "The Siren of Scuba," *Life*, June 1987, pp. 46–51. A close-up look at Sylvia's love of SCUBA diving.

Hawkes, Graham S. and Philip J. Ballou, "The Ocean Everest Concept: A Versatile Manned Submersible for Full Ocean Depth," *Marine Technology Society Journal*, June 1990, pp. 79 86. An engineer's perspective on Ocean Everest.

Idyll, C. P. *Abyss—The Deep Sea and the Creatures That Live in It* (New York: Thomas Y. Crowell, 1964). A classic presentation of the deep sea, and an especially good look at the creatures that inhabit the depths.

Lee, Annette Hannon., "Earle of the Oceans," *Florida State Magazine*, summer 1990, pp. 8–11. Good background on Sylvia and her education.

Markle, Sandra. "The Deep Rover and Other Ways to Explore the Ocean Frontier," *Instructor and Teacher*, January 1985, pp. 81–83.

Pope, Gregory T., "Deep Flight," *Popular Mechanics*, April 1990, pp. 70–72. Technical background on Deep Flight and Ocean Everest.

The Rand McNally Atlas of the Oceans (New York: Rand McNally, 1977). A detailed look at underwater mountain chains, trenches, and other oceanographic information.

National Geographic Society, *Sylvia Earle: Portrait of an Aquanaut*, video, 1987.

White, Wallace. "Profiles—Her Deepness," *New Yorker*, July 3, 1989, pp. 41–66. A comprehensive biographical sketch of Sylvia and her accomplishments.

Suggested Reading

Adler, David. *Our Amazing Ocean*. Mahwah, NJ: Troll Associates, 1983.

Asimov, Isaac. *How Did We Find Out about Life in the Deep Sea?* New York: Walker, 1981.

Ballard, Robert D. *Exploring the Titanic*. New York: Scholastic, 1990.

Blair, Carvel. *Exploring the Sea: Oceanography Today*. New York: Random House, 1986.

Bramwell, Martyn. *Oceanography—Science Frontiers*. New York: Hamstead Press, 1989.

Brindze, Ruth. *All about Undersea Exploration*. New York: Random House, 1964.

Center for Environmental Education Staff. *The Ocean Book: Aquarium & Seaside Activities & Ideas for All Ages*. New York: Wiley, 1989.

Embry, Lynn. *Scientific Encounters of the Mysterious Sea*. Carthage, IL: Good Apple, 1987.

Fine, John C. *Oceans in Peril*. New York: Macmillan, 1987.

Gilbreath, Alice. *River in the Ocean: The Story of the Gulf Stream*. Minneapolis, MN: Dillon, 1986.

Hargreaves, Pat. *Seas & Oceans*, 8 vols., Silver Burdett, Lexington, MA: 1981.

Heintze, Carl. *The Bottom of the Sea & Beyond*, New York: Lodestar Books, 1975.

Matthews, Rupert. *Record Breakers of the Sea*. Mahwah, NJ: Troll Associates, 1989.

McCoy, Lois, and Floyd McCoy. *Science under Sail: The Story of Oceanography*. New York: Henry Holt, 1985.

Moore, Chris. *Oceans*. New York: Puffin Bks, 1988.

Morris, R. *Ocean Life* Mysteries & Marvels Series, Tulsa, OK. Usborne-Hayes, 1983.

Polking, Kirk. *Oceans of the World: Our Essential Resource*. New York: Putnam, 1983.

Robinson, W. Wright. *Incredible Facts about the Ocean: The Land Below, the Life Within*, vol. 2. Minneapolis, MN: Dillon, 1987.

Sabin, Louis. *Wonders of the Sea*. Mahwah, NJ: Troll Associates, 1982.

Seddon, Tony, and Jill Bailey. *Physical World*. New York: Doubleday, 1987.

Sibbald, Jean. *Homes in the Sea: From the Shore to the Deep*. Minneapolis, MN: Dillon, 1986.

Sibbald, Jean. *Sea Babies: New Life in the Ocean*. Minneapolis, MN: Dillon, 1986.

Simon, Seymour. *How to Be an Ocean Scientist in Your Own Home*. New York: Harper & Row Junior Books, 1988.

Sipiera, Paul. *I Can Be an Oceanographer*. Chicago, IL: Childrens Press, 1987.

Time-Life. *Life in the Water*. A Child's First Library of Learning, Alexandria, VA: Time-Life, 1989.

Whipple, A. B. *Restless Oceans*. Alexandria, VA: Time-Life, 1983.

Index

Japan Trench

Marianas Trench

Challenger Deep

Yap Trench

Philippine Trench

Java Trench

INDIAN OCEAN

Sea level
656 feet (200 m) below sea level
13,123 feet (4,000 m) below sea level
22,966 feet (7,000 m) below sea level